Text copyright © 2007 by Cris Peterson

Photographs copyright © 2007 by David R. Lundquist,

with the exception of the aerial farm shots on pages 9 and 27,

courtesy of Dairyland Power, La Crosse, Wisconsin

All rights reserved

Boyds Mills Press, Inc.

815 Church Street

Honesdale, Pennsylvania 18431

Printed in China

CIP data is available

First edition

Book design by Amy Drinker, Aster Designs

The text of this book is set in 15-point New Century Schoolbook

10 9 8 7 6 5 4 3 2 1

Clarabelle

Making Milk and So Much More

Cris Peterson

Photographs by
David R. Lundquist

Boyds Mills Press

Honesdale, Pennsylvania

*With thanks to the
Heer family of Norswiss Farms*
—C.P.

*To my mother, Mardelle,
for her continued and loving support*
—D.R.L.

Just over the crest of
a freshly mown alfalfa field
in a huge white-roofed dairy
barn lives Clarabelle....

Clarabelle's black fuzzy ears jut out at right angles from the sides of her knobby head. Her soft brown eyes are framed in black and separated by a wide band of white that runs from the top of her head to her muzzle. Her angular body is covered with huge black spots that look like splashes of ink. A few pieces of grain and a stray alfalfa leaf or two stick to her whiskery nose, which spends a good part of each day burrowed in a pile of feed.

Clarabelle is a Holstein dairy cow. She lives with twelve hundred other cows on a family farm called Norswiss owned by Sam and Josh's parents and grandparents. The barn sprawls across the top of a rolling hill in northern Wisconsin surrounded by fields of corn and hay. Thick groves of oak and maple trees dot the landscape, providing habitat for deer and other wildlife that feed on some of the corn grown for the cows. Sam and Josh, along with their two older brothers, help at the dairy when they're not in school.

Clarabelle is big and bony. She weighs nearly fifteen hundred pounds—about as much as a soccer team of second-graders with the coaches thrown in for good measure—and she's almost as tall as Josh and Sam's dad. Each year she gives birth to a calf that weighs about one hundred pounds. Then she produces milk that is bottled for drinking or made into cheese, ice cream, yogurt, and other dairy products.

hay

corn

To make all that milk, Clarabelle eats heaping piles of hay, corn, and soybean meal. The seven tons of feed she chomps down every year is enough to fill a bedroom to the ceiling three times. Her amazing four-compartment stomach recycles leftover food and fiber products such as brewer's grain, sugar-beet pulp, and cottonseed. Finally, the manure she creates during all this manufacturing helps generate electricity. It also provides fresh bedding for the cow stalls as well as fertilizer for the crops grown to feed her. You could say that Clarabelle is a four-footed factory.

cottonseed

corn silage

Before Clarabelle can produce milk, she has to give birth to a calf. At Norswiss, calves are born every day of the year, and on the day Clarabelle's calf is born, four other cows give birth, too. Cows don't usually need assistance with calving, but Josh and Sam happen to be helping in the barn when Clarabelle and two other cows calve.

Within minutes of the big event, the newborns begin to struggle to their feet as each one endures enthusiastic cleaning by its mother's sandpapery tongue. Snuggled in the deep straw of the maternity pen, the calves are fed bottles of warm, creamy first milk by Sam and Josh.

After giving birth, Clarabelle really goes to work. Three times a day beginning at seven o'clock in the morning, she and the other cows from her pen trundle down a lane toward the milking center at Norswiss. Clarabelle waits her turn to enter a stall in the center, where a worker cleans and prepares her for milking. She stands quietly while a milking machine is attached to her four teats.

inside the milking center

inside the milking center

Music floats from a boom box near the entry to the milking
center as Clarabelle stands placidly chewing her cud. All the
pumps and motors that run the milking equipment are located
in the basement beneath the center so the equipment stays clean
and the center remains quiet for the cows. Whirring fans blow
fresh air through the building.

As soon as the machine is attached to Clarabelle, she starts giving milk. In less time than it takes for an average kid to eat a bowl of cereal, she gives nearly five gallons—enough to pour on 160 bowls of cereal. The milk then travels from the milking machine through a pipeline to a refrigerated cooler, where it is kept fresh and cold.

milking machine

the basement beneath the milking center

Each of the coolers that Josh and Sam are perched on holds six thousand gallons of milk, enough to make thousands of pounds of cheese or pails of ice cream. Twice each day, a tanker truck pulls up to the milking center and the driver transfers a full cooler of milk to his truck. He dips out a sample of each load to test for bacteria, and butterfat, and protein, and to make sure it is clean and pure. Then the milk is hauled to a cheese factory nearby. The empty cooler is automatically washed and sanitized.

To manufacture all that creamy white milk, Clarabelle has to eat a lot. She stands at the manger and eats several bushels of feed at one time. Then she lies down and brings some of it back up into her mouth and chews it like bubble gum. This chewing is called rumination, or "cud chewing," and it's the process that allows a cow to obtain energy from plants. Clarabelle spends four out of every six hours eating and rechewing her feed. Stuff that humans could never digest travels through her four-compartment stomach and breaks down into nutritious food. All that chewing makes her produce nearly thirty gallons of saliva a day. That's a lot of drool!

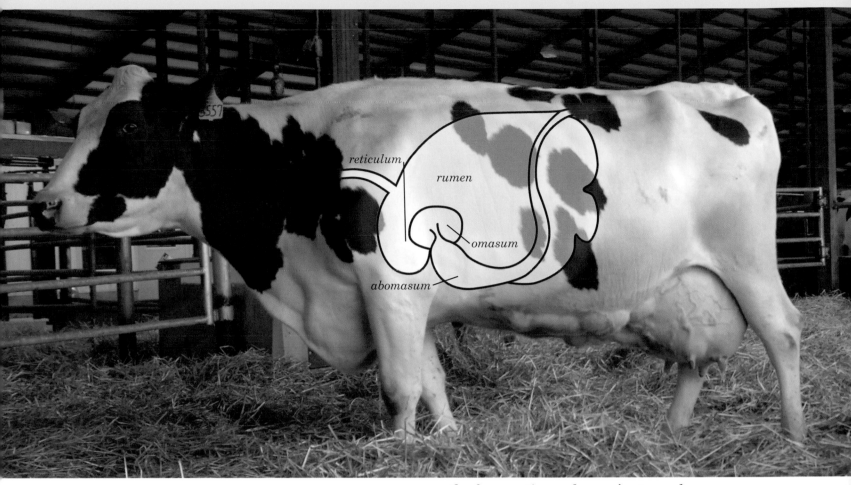

the four sections of a cow's stomach

The rumen is the largest of the four compartments in
Clarabelle's stomach. It holds twenty-five gallons of material,
or about as much as your bathtub holds when it's half-full.
The rumen works like a huge churning, bubbling vat where
bacteria and other microorganisms break down the tough,
chewy feed into nutrients Clarabelle can use to make milk.

Mountains of chopped corn and alfalfa silage are stored at Norswiss, ready to feed to the cows. Silvery bins of soybean meal, ground corn, and other dry feeds are lined up next to a giant truck scale. Every day a worker scoops up piles of silage with a machine that has fat wheels and looks like an overgrown go-cart. The machine is called a telehandler because its telescoping bucket scoops up each ingredient, lifts it high into the air, and dumps it into a mixer truck. All the good stuff for Clarabelle's balanced diet is measured into the machine and tossed like an enormous garden salad.

The mixture is specially formulated by a dairy nutritionist to meet the needs of all the cows at Norswiss. The recipe appears on the computer screen in the mixer truck and in the barn office. The daily feast is delivered right in front of Clarabelle and her hungry herdmates when they come back from the milking center.

But before Clarabelle returns to her meal, a worker scrapes the manure from her pen. The cow stalls are cleaned, and fresh bedding made from manure is blown from a bedding shooter into the stalls to keep the cows comfortable.

Cow stalls full of manure?! That sounds pretty yucky.
At Norswiss, a complicated bunch of equipment and storage
vats located just beyond Clarabelle's barn turn manure into
clean bedding, electricity, and fertilizer for the soil on the farm.

The system is called an anaerobic digester—a fancy name for a group of separators, tanks, and converters in which microscopic bacteria eat cow manure and in the process create methane. Methane is a flammable gas that is used to power a generator. The generator makes electricity, which is sold to the local power company. The leftover solids from the digester are used as bedding for the cows. At Norswiss, the electrical generator runs day and night, creating enough electricity to power four hundred homes.

digester monitoring station

bedding from the digester

Sam and Josh with their father and grandfather, looking at diagrams of how the digester works

Josh and Sam's dairy farm is a big operation. Many people besides their family work there. They help cultivate hundreds of acres of crops to grow all the feed needed for Clarabelle and her twelve hundred herdmates. Each cow on the farm will produce enough milk in her lifetime to feed a family of four for seventeen years.

But Clarabelle is more than just a mooing, chewing food factory. She's part of Josh and Sam's family heritage that goes back several generations. Without knowing it, she and the rest of the cows at Norswiss create food, renewable energy, and a successful business. Each day as Clarabelle ambles down the lane from the milking center, buries her big, wet nose into a pile of fragrant feed, and spends hours chewing her cud, her remarkable system produces milk—and so much more.

Glossary

Alfalfa—a plant grown as a forage crop to feed dairy cows

Bacteria—tiny one-celled organisms that play many roles in nature. On a dairy farm, various types of bacteria can work to break down plant material in a cow's stomach or in an anaerobic digester. Other bacteria can cause milk to sour.

Butterfat—the fat contained in milk

Cud—previously swallowed food that is returned to the mouth and chewed again

Dairy nutritionist—a scientist who specializes in formulating a properly balanced diet for cows

Fertilizer—material given to plants usually by adding it to the soil, providing nutrients that will improve plant growth

First milk—the protein-rich milk, or colostrum, produced by a cow just after she gives birth

Manger—the area or trough where cows eat

Manure—waste material from animals

Maternity pen—special area where cows give birth

Methane—a flammable substance found in natural gas and formed by the breakdown of plant materials

Protein—an essential nutrient found in milk and in all living cells

Silage—chopped and fermented corn or alfalfa plants that are stored in covered piles or silos and used as cow feed

Soybean meal—high-protein grain fed to dairy cows

Stalls—individual spaces for cows to rest

Teats—nipples through which cow milk is extracted